BRITAIN IN PICTURES
THE BRITISH PEOPLE IN PICTURES

ENGLISH NOVELISTS

GENERAL EDITOR
W. J. TURNER

The Editor is most grateful to all those who have
so kindly helped in the selection of illustrations
especially to officials of the various public
Museums Libraries and Galleries and
to all others who have generously
allowed pictures and MSS
to be reproduced

ENGLISH NOVELISTS

ELIZABETH BOWEN

WITH
8 PLATES IN COLOUR
AND
16 ILLUSTRATIONS IN
BLACK & WHITE

COLLINS · 14 ST. JAMES'S PLACE · LONDON

MCMXLVII

PRODUCED BY
ADPRINT LIMITED LONDON

FIRST PUBLISHED 1942
FOURTH IMPRESSION 1947

PRINTED IN GREAT BRITAIN BY
CLARKE & SHERWELL LTD NORTHAMPTON
ON MELLOTEX BOOK PAPER MADE BY
TULLIS RUSSELL & CO LTD MARKINCH SCOTLAND

LIST OF ILLUSTRATIONS

PLATES IN COLOUR

BLACK AND WHITE ILLUSTRATIONS

THE English novel, from its beginning on, has been the subject of so much critical writing that one may feel there remains little to add. Its characteristics have been defined; its development has been noted ; influences upon it have been traced. In so far as all this may enlarge our pleasure in reading, we owe thanks to the critic. I do, however, see one danger—that too much information about great novels may make us less spontaneous in our approach to them—though they offer entrancing subjects for study, they were in the first place written to be enjoyed. It would be sad to regard as lecture-room subjects books that were meant to be part of life. As things are, are our classical English novels not often left to the honour of our high-up shelves, where they receive little other attention than the periodic dusting of their tops, while that place for which their lively authors designed them, the place on the book-table by the arm-chair, is taken by modern writers whose chief attraction is that we have not yet been required to find them "good" ?

We lose much if we ignore, or honour in name only, so living a part of the English heritage. And now, when the English spirit stands at its full height, to do so would be a double loss. England's past in art, as well as in history, has helped to build up her heroic To-day. It is natural to want our writers beside us as we face this new phase of human experience. And painters and writers, however long dead, however far back their place in actual time, remain, in their living art, our contemporaries. Their domain is always the domain of living men ; it is to us, the living, that they are speaking now. This is as true of the novelists as it is of the painters or poets—as true, but not so easily recognised. Why ? Because while in painter or poet we expect the sublime (or timeless), in the novelist we expect the familiar, the day-to-day. The novel, we feel, should keep close to life. Whatever seems unlikely is fatal to it. The novelist must be a man of his own day—and, as that day of his gives place to another, and as that other

gives place to our own, may we not feel that he depicts only what was, so that his judgments seem to lose their point ? How, the would-be reader may ask, can I find the familiar, the convincing, the likely, in a novel written two hundred years ago ?

The answer, of course, is that while novelists must belong to their own day, the great novelist is not confined by that. Poor novels do pass away with their time ; they pass because they concerned themselves only with the ephemeral parts of human experience, not with its lasting essentials. But in the great novel, we recognise those essentials that run through all experience, independent of time. We may, in fact, see for the first time what those essentials are. We see, too, why fundamentally men and women have changed so little. In a novel that has been great enough to survive the years, we shall find very little that is unfamiliar or queer. Any feeling of queerness evaporates in the course of the first pages. Differences of speech, costume, habits, manners do not affect us as we had thought they would : instead, we are made aware of the underlying likeness of life then to life as it is to-day.

The English novel, the novel proper, began in the Age of Reason—in fact, at a time when people thought for themselves—and reason has continued to be its godmother. But the genius that gave the novel its truth and life is, at the same time, something beyond the scope of reason ; a sort of romantic miracle. In the course of the English novel, since its beginning, the English have continued to show and to see themselves— islanders, haughty, puzzled, at once saved and graced by a comicality to which they are not blind. The novel has been an overflow of a number of English people's feeling for their own life—and, also, it voices a criticism. It is as givers of one particular sort of pleasure, and inspirers of a particular sort of interest, that I shall discuss the English novelists. While I shall hope to be fair, I cannot avoid the influence of my own taste. I read for pleasure, and it must be remembered that I write as a pleasure-seeker and not a judge.

OF the English novel, before the eighteenth century, there were several curious false dawns. These attempts at the novel have a sort of interest for their own sakes. In the England of Queen Elizabeth the demand for entertainment was general, and the arts made a noble response to it. English drama then came, as we know, to its greatest height—and, as the mass of the people could still not read, drama continued to be the popular art. Writers who wrote anything other than plays addressed themselves to a literate, elegant upper class, and Elizabethans who did experiment in the novel either shared or flattered the Court's taste. The way was prepared for story-tellers by an existing vogue for Italian tales—this not the first nor the last of invasions of foreign fancy

JOSEPH ANDREWS AND MR. ADAMS WITH FANNY AT THE WAYSIDE INN
An illustration to *Joseph Andrews* by Henry Fielding
Water colour by Thomas Hearne
By courtesy of Walker's Galleries, London

MR. BURCHELL RESCUING SOPHIA PRIMROSE
An illustration to the *Vicar of Wakefield* by Oliver Goldsmith
Water colour by Thomas Hearne
By courtesy of Walker's Galleries, London

that have reached the English shore. First by late-Renaissance Italy then by France, the English have been at once englamoured and shocked. By the time John Lyly, a Kentish man born in 1553, brought out his *Euphues*, translations from the Italian had set up a pretty high standard in artifice. Of this Lyly was so careful not to fall short that he decidedly over-reached himself ; also, he gave his first story a foreign scene. In *Euphues, the Anatomy of Wit*, published in 1579 and followed a year later by *Euphues and his England*, all late-Renaissance influences appear. There are great flights of discourse ; everything is kept at the highest possible level above the everyday. The hero Euphues, his romantic friend Philautus and the lady who proves false to them both, leave few subjects of gallant òr philosophic interest untouched. In the second half of the story the high-minded Euphues visits England, and comments on much that he finds there. *Euphues* had an immediate, hectic success in circles for which it was designed. But the success was brief—against Lyly's wrought-up style, with its hollow elegances, strained ingenuities, and overload of classical references there came a revulsion that was severe. Common sense began to assert itself, and enthusiasts felt that they had been fooled. Ridicule swept away *Euphues*—which is now chiefly remembered as having added a word to the English vocabulary. . . . The *Arcadia* of Sir Philip Sidney (born at Penshurst, 1554) fared a good deal better, as it deserved. The *Arcadia* is a sort of sustained dream, and also it has the consistency of a book written to please oneself—for Sir Philip, by himself for some time at his sister's house in the country, undertook the *Arcadia* for this reason alone. Courtier-soldier, traveller, lover, poet and man of the world, Sir Philip brought to his narrative prose-poem unusual feeling and innate stylishness. In the *Arcadia*, pairs of lovers wander in the seclusion of a pastoral world—though on this is imposed a complex plot. When, in 1590, four years after its author's death in battle, the *Arcadia* appeared (against his wishes, for he had asked that it should be burned), it went straight to the hearts of the *beau monde*, to whom, in the heated pressure of Court life, pastoral distances seemed idyllic—in fact, the theme of Arden was here. Though Sidney's lovers show less spirit than Shakespeare's, the breeze from *Arcadia* continued to blow sweet ; and, not in itself deeply original, for pastorals had already been done abroad, the book was to be in its turn followed by a number of imitations in this genre.

John Greene (born in Norwich about 1560) belongs with the rakes and the realists. When he left Cambridge for London it was not to come to Court but to pick up a living by pamphleteering and the writing of plays. His trade was tough, his companions low. In this milieu, a gust of contempt for the unreal made him discard the *Euphues* influence under which his own first story, *Mamillia*, had been penned at Cambridge in 1583. So his succeeding stories, though still romantic, have that progressive strength that comes from a truer view. But more important were his pamphlets, that, in story-interest and length, began to approach short novels ; in these he broke away from the courtly idea and wrote of the stinking, stewing London he knew—whether fine nostrils liked it or not. In this break with flattery and illusion, Greene came to be followed by "ingenuous, ingenious, fluent, facetious Thomas Nash" (born at Lowestoft, 1567), who also developed the satiric attacking style.

So the Elizabethan period closes with two very opposite tendencies in the air. And a place for the narrative that was to become the novel had been at least made—though now that place was to stay empty for some time. With the end of Elizabeth's reign some creative urge subsided, and experiments came to a standstill.

IN the seventeenth century, in which so much happened, little worth speaking of happened to the novel. John Bunyan was, it is true, to give, with his *Pilgrim's Progress* (1678), one of our grandest examples of story-telling. But first, the theatre kept its hold over the people—though drama was in a state of noisy decline ; then, battles and metaphysics came with the Civil War. In 1642 the Puritan parliament closed the theatres, and, to escape from an oversevere world, pleasure-loving society turned to reading, and sought again—this time as an anodyne—the seductions of the imported romance. France now supplied the demand. Long-winded reconstructions of chivalry helped the ladies and gentlemen of the defeated faction through the Commonwealth gloom, and when the Restoration brought out the sun again the French romances could more freely circulate. For the English, the Frenchmen could hardly write fast enough—and quite soon English imitators sprang up. One cannot praise, and need not discuss, the results. However, with regard to the novel, the century had not a quite barren close : in 1692 one exquisite tale, *Incognita*, came from Congreve the dramatist. But the theatre was entirely to claim Congreve—it was having another tremendous boom. Literature, apart from dramatic art, was to be the domain of a few exquisite but rather detached minds. Vigorous invention and curiosity went, rather, to scientific research.

Story-telling, however, had one more likely recruit in the person of Mrs. Aphra Behn. Though there were unkind judgments of this lady, she had one great merit : she wrote from experience. She had lived abroad, and she had lived to the full. Though subject to flights and foolishness, she had energy—more energy, some people considered, than was becoming in her sex. There was a tendency, due to last a long time, to regard professional novel-writing as an immodest, too dashing occupation for women ; in fact, well on into the nineteenth century gentlewomen whose novels found publication remained anonymous, or used pen-names. When, in 1698, Mrs. Behn's two best-known novels, *Oroonoko* and *The Fair Jilt*, appeared, she had already been dead some years. *Oroonoko*, with its

negro hero, put out that idea of the noble savage that Rousseau was to make popular with a romantic age. Aphra Behn is at least a landmark : the rest of the sub-heroic nonsense of her period vanished, leaving behind for the novel only a bad name.

The seventeenth century, all the same, produced the England that was to produce the novel. Out of the Civil War a new kind of English self-consciousness had been born. Social thought was already upon its way. The new interest in science had made people objective, curious, analytical. The complexity of the spirit of man was recognised—and, with this, his tie to the natural world. Most important, a new class had come into conscious power—the middle class, self-reliant, anti-feudal and sturdy. This class was to ask from art something new. The courtly idea had gone for ever, to be succeeded by the democratic idea.

DISABUSED, critical, liking fact and inclined to rate fancy low, why should the eighteenth century have given birth to the novel ? For some time, indeed, the brilliant essayists reigned. But it was two of these, Steele and Addison, who by their sketches in the *Tatler* (1709-1711) and the *Spectator* (1711-1712) made a step forward towards the novel by creating interest in character—or, should one say, heightening interest that had begun to exist? The members of Mr. Bickerstaff's Club (in the *Tatler*) and Sir Roger de Coverley and his friends (in the *Spectator*) stepped from print into life with an utter convincingness. These were individual people ; no longer the dreary "types" who had dominated the English story and play. Only continuous narrative of their actions was needed to make Sir Roger and the others into characters in a novel—but this their creators did not choose to supply.

Daniel Defoe (a butcher's son born in London in 1660) perceived character, though he put action first : though what straighter approach to character could there be than the story of a man alone with himself ?—and *Robinson Crusoe*, Defoe's first great work of fiction, was published in 1719. Defoe started late in fiction but not in writing : pamphlets, verses, satires, treatises had for years poured from his ready pen. Disgrace, a stand in the pillory and the loss of his business (he had started a brick kiln at Tilbury) had, by following on his double-edged pamphlet, *The Shortest Way with the Dissenters* (1702), already shown him his pen's danger—and power. He paid high for a laugh that no one else had enjoyed. When Defoe returned to his craft it was in a desperate spirit ; starvation faced him and his family. By this time, however, he had the public taped ; he resolved to make profit out of its gullibility, and the possibilities of fiction, to this end, at once presented themselves to him. He wrote up the case of a Mrs. Veal who after her death appeared to a friend in Canterbury, and he did not fail to put Mrs. Veal across. Defoe developed two great assets : plausibility and a superb style, at once matter-of-fact and evocative. His English has, to my mind, never been bettered : it is the ideal narrator's prose. After *Robinson Crusoe* came, in 1721, *Moll Flanders*—a great fascinating acute short book on no account to be missed by anybody. The bad beauty who names it is immortal : never was a life lived with more style. *Colonel Jack* came in 1722, and *Roxana* in 1724.

Everything that Defoe wrote reads as true. (He carried this so far as to be able to fake memory in his *Journal of the Plague Year*.) He sets up for us the important rule that a story-teller must be believed. It is true that he tested his plausibility on no subject so fantastic as that of the *Gulliver's Travels* (to give the book its short name) of Dean Swift—published in 1726. Swift's vast satiric imagination did not disdain, in *Gulliver's Travels*, the minutest details that would convince. Though the head may say to the reader, You know, this could not have happened, the imagination answers, It surely did. We see—and so we believe. In fact, to Defoe and

Swift the English novel owes its powerful start. We have come to the end of the false dawns. The novel could only come into power when it took account of the forces of common sense.

Two elements of the novel were, thus, waiting—likely and living character, likely and living plot. But a third was needed, to merge these two. What was this ? —interest in human relationships. The tract in which men and men, or men and women, affect, act on and conflict with each other was still waiting to be explored. It had been accepted that it is from a man's character that his actions spring. One had now to see the effect that one man or woman, by acting in character, had on the action or character of another. It had, too, to be seen that human behaviour seldom follows a set course (or course planned in the head), being often deflected by accidents. The nature and cause of the accidents that deflect behaviour might be called the stuff of the novel. Most often, these are psychological : conflicting desires between two people are more important than a tempest or a coach being overturned. One can see why the novel must have love interest—though in as wide a sense as you like.

And the novelist had to accept a fact known to his readers—that behaviour, however wide its zigzags, very seldom goes over certain set bounds. What sets these bounds ? Society, what one might call the world of the everyone-else, that world in which each man or woman, by being born, takes up his or her inherited place. The relation of a man to society is an integral part of the concept of any novel. In the eighteenth century, the idea of society crystallised : the novel, in fact, was the product of a great social age. A man's relationship to society was seen as his first important and human one—he might fly from or defy society by becoming a hermit or vagabond, but he could not ignore it, for its existence gave him his meaning and shape. It was seen, I think rightly, that the fact that human beings do not live for themselves only, in vacuo, makes them more rather than less interesting.

This new contemplative interest in human beings was not on the level of poetry : sublimity played little part in it. The medium for its expression was prose narrative—but this would have to contain much. England being now ripe for the novel, the novel came. The public sprang to meet *Pamela*, published in 1740.

SAMUEL RICHARDSON, the middle-aged London printer who became the author of *Pamela*, was a pursy, not interesting little man. Born in 1689, son of a joiner in Derbyshire, he had received a limited education, had come to London as an apprentice, done well and married his master's daughter. His experience of the world was limited—as some absurdities in *Pamela* show.

His life was troubled more by domestic griefs—there were many deaths in his family—than by emotional storms. His personal tameness makes all the odder his faculty—one is entitled to call it genius—for the analysis of the human heart. He is said, as a prim cold-blooded little boy of thirteen, to have been the confidant of a group of young ladies for whom he indited love-letters ; and this precocious knowledge of love, at an age before one feels love, may account for much. Certainly, given the masculine temperament of the eighteenth century, Richardson's knowledge of women is extraordinary. His detractors might say that he spied on women rather than felt for them—certainly Richardson's heroines arouse (as he intended) solicitude rather than desire. (Fielding's heroines, on the other hand, are desirable before everything.) In *Pamela*, marred, as I say, by absurdities and more than a little shocking in its success philosophy, Richardson no more than foreshadows his coming powers. The *réclame* that *Pamela* gained him, the many new doors that opened to the successful author, he was artist enough to put to a good use. Also he learned a lesson from the experience of having *Pamela* ridiculed—of Fielding's ruthlessness I have yet to speak. In the eight years between *Pamela* and *Clarissa*, Richardson came out of his chrysalis. *Pamela* is a slight story brilliantly told. Of *Clarissa*, at the end of two hundred years, we may say : this remains one of the finest novels we have.

But *Pamela* is more than an innovation. To what can we trace the charm of this shocking book ? Partly to the unerringness with which the sense of predicament is sustained. Partly to the vivacity of the dialogue. Partly to the intimacy of the manner—the book is written in letters, but it is more than that. Richardson not only adored detail but had an unfailing sense of its place in art.

Those who do not like him find his atmosphere too indoor—claustrophobic, in fact. It is true that his characters are constricted by their emotions into a tiny, oppressive world. . . . Pamela Andrews, little waiting-maid of fifteen, adorably pretty, a chaste minx, is left, by the death of her mistress and patroness, exposed to the evil designs of that lady's son, Mr. B. From the slender defences she clings to at his Bedfordshire country house, Mr. B. whisks Pamela off to his still more lonely estate in Lincolnshire.

"About eight o'clock at night" (Pamela writes to her parents, for whose peace of mind she seems to have no regard) "we entered the courtyard of this handsome, large, old and lonely mansion, that looks made for solitude and mischief, as I thought by its appearance, with all its brown nodding horrors of lofty elms and pines about it. Here, I said to myself, I fear is to be the scene of my ruin. . . ."

Crude is hardly the word for Mr. B's goings-on. And he is not even high-spirited. There comes the crucial occasion when Pamela's virtue is only saved by her collapse into alarming fits. Mr. B., unnerved, thinks again : he ends by proposing marriage. Whereupon, Pamela, idealist in behaviour, accepts the husband she has up to now considered a mean, inestimable young man. The book's morality founders on this rock, and

14

SAMUEL RICHARDSON 1689-1761
Oil painting by Joseph Highmore

Pamela's bridal prosperity, though described with spirit, leaves one cold. The book, with unconscious cynicism, is sub-titled *Virtue Rewarded*.

One stands dumb, all the same, before the accomplishment of this first English novel. So did the world of its day. But the moral flaw in the book was perceived, without mercy, by at least one mind. It was on *Pamela's* weakness that Fielding pounced. Henry Fielding, Richardson's junior by eighteen years, was born to many advantages that the printer, through no fault of his own, lacked. Fielding was a gentleman, a wit, a rake and a scholar. Born at his grandfather's country house near Glastonbury in 1707, educated at Eton, he had found himself with remarkably little money and had been by turns journalist, playwright, barrister. By the time he read *Pamela* he was tough, poised, satiric—but something more. The full possibilities of this new form, the novel, may or may not at first have appeared to him. We know that he set out on his *Joseph Andrews* in a spirit of pure burlesque.

15

In *Joseph Andrews*, published 1742, Fielding gives Richardson's Pamela Andrews a brother Joseph, virtuous as herself and exposed to equal difficulties. The handsome young footman too well pleases his widowed employer's eye. His employer is Lady Booby, the aunt by marriage of Richardson's sinister Mr. B. Mr. B.—it could not have been more annoying —is thus made to enter Fielding's pages as young Mr. Booby, with Pamela as his exceedingly snobbish bride. Richardson called *Joseph Andrews* "a lewd and ungenerous engrafture"—and probably did not stop at that. But neither did Fielding stop at his burlesque—the novel ran far away from it, to our eternal gain. Joseph may be the hero, but he is soon eclipsed by the outsize figure of Parson Adams—Joseph's friend and patron, with his big heart, big family and big fist, his erudition and innocence, his Christian humility and his hot temper, his astounding get-up, optimism and constantly mislaid and forgotten horse. When Joseph flies from Lady Booby's in London, he meets Parson Adams, who is looking for him. Fanny, Joseph's young village love, has also left home to seek him—so these three range the country together on a much-interrupted journey home. And what country they travel, and in how roaring a spirit! If solicitude is the note of Richardson's novels, zest is the note of Fielding's. Strongly under the influence of Cervantes, he loved movement, the fantastic, the outdoor. In this first book we feel the author getting into his stride. Fielding had more to carry than Richardson, and so the content of every one of his novels is always a little more than their form will hold. But his very prodigality is superb. He is the masculine writer par excellence; in no other Englishman who has written has the masculine quality been so pure. Among the other sex one might say that only Jane Austen has been his counterpart—she wrought her own femininity into an art as tempered and as dispassionate.

On Richardson, the umbrage occasioned by *Joseph Andrews* had been having a far from bad effect, for in 1748 he published *Clarissa*—which one might call the corrective to *Pamela*. Here is the same situation, but with another approach—and from it breathes the real horror *Pamela* lacks. In her bitter struggle with Lovelace, Clarissa Harlowe has—unlike Pamela in her struggle with Mr. B.—nothing to gain. She is a young beauty, born to her own position, till lately adored by her proud family, and asking no more than to go on being tranquilly happy in her country home, Harlowe Place. In fact, she asks no more than to keep herself—but this is what Lovelace hates her to do. Threatened at home by an odious marriage, Clarissa is tricked into flight with Lovelace, who has continued to offer her a protection that should be completely disinterested. No sooner is she upon the road with him than he justifies her instinctive mistrust, and by a series of outrages breaks down—here is the core of the tragedy—the love for him she had been so ready to feel. In his hatred of what he calls her pride—though this hatred is knit up with a desperate love—he makes

A GIPSY TELLING THE FORTUNES OF PAMELA AND MRS. JEWKES

An illustration to *Pamela* by Samuel Richardson

Oil painting attributed to J. F. Nollekens after the engraving by H. F. Gravelot

YORICK, THE MONK AND MADAME L— IN THE INN COURTYARD AT CALAIS
An illustration to *A Sentimental Journey* by Laurence Sterne
Water colour by Adam Buck

her suffer every abuse of the power from which she is unable to free herself. Clarissa, in the end, dies, but dies with her colours flying : though Lovelace, having drugged her, has once stolen her body, they both know that her spirit remains intact. Steadily, she has refused the marriage he offers: she cannot marry without love, cannot love without honour, and cannot honour the man who, by every action, has ruined his (not her own) honour in her eyes. One may say that, in this stand she took up, Clarissa was not only high above Pamela but very much in advance of her own time—in which (with a cynicism that was to last) marriage was supposed "to make everything all right." Clarissa may well have been found exacting. Was she, perhaps, proud ? Her sense of her own pathos does a little alienate us from her—"A young creature like I am," she often says.

The story is (like *Pamela*) told in letters : Clarissa and Lovelace each have confidants of their own sex. But the letters read more like journals : there are pages and pages of brilliant dialogue. Also, a circle of other characters is made to surround the hating lovers—most notable is the figure of Anna Howe, Clarissa's high-spirited, gallant girl friend, who has Mr. Hickman for quiet *fiancé*. But the outstanding figure of the book is not Clarissa ; it is Lovelace himself—the brilliant neurotic rake. The pathological complexities of Lovelace, the extravagance of his reactions are, I say firmly, absolutely convincing; I say this firmly because, by some critics, Lovelace has been denounced as "impossible."

Clarissa has a compactness (in spite of its great length) and a saturation in its own moral atmosphere to which few novels have so completely attained. It has a convincingness nothing can break through. . . . In 1753 Richardson followed up with *Sir Charles Grandison*, the tale of a model baronet and his ladies, but after *Clarissa* this lacks emotional power and seems diffuse, artificial and slow. France as well as England wept over *Clarissa*—but France was shocked by Fielding's ultra-English *Tom Jones*. It is interesting to compare Fielding's masterpiece—published in 1749, one year after *Clarissa*—with Richardson's. Fielding's conscience—or call it morality—was a thing tempered out of his own furious living ; Richardson's conscience remained a theory—though a theory brought to a fine point. The predicament of the conscience is the real preoccupation of *Tom Jones*, in spite of the novel's lordly, spacious, picaresque overlay and its rough-house scenes. Tom Jones, the handsome foundling, is a bad lad who constantly disappoints the squire who brought him up and deviates from his ideal love for Sophia. Circumstances combine to treat Tom hardly, and he hardily does what he can with them. Turned out by the squire, he rides the country with his self-seeking Sancho, Partridge, and, coming to London to seek Sophia, is more than half embroiled by all the wiles of the town. In Sophia Western, who "with all the gentleness which a woman can have, had all the spirit which she ought to have," Fielding creates the first of the English novel's adorable heroines. The book is, again, pre-eminent in its comedy characters : to have sat through Hamlet with Partridge, as Tom did, can have been only second in pleasure to sitting through *Hamlet* with Miss Bates. And there is Squire Western, baited in argument by his sister, that blue-stocking and snob, till "Damn Milton!" roars the suffering Squire. Squire Western remains the prototype of one very marked kind of landed English commoner. "I hate all lords," he says simply, "they are a parcel of courtiers and Hanoverians, and I will have nothing to do with them." That is that. The other type—more thoughtful but as feudal—is represented by Squire Allworthy. "Love," says Squire Allworthy, to the (apparently) erring Jenny Jones, "however much we may corrupt and pervert its meaning . . . remains a rational passion."

This idea—or ideal—of the rational passion is strong in Fielding, as it is in his race, as it was in his century. It had even been, in a sense, to this ideal that Richardson's bewildered Clarissa clung. And the idea of love on this plane has continued to rule the English novel—one may say that, to an extent, it has limited it. The French and the Russians have been left to explore love's inherent principles of disorder and pain.

Fielding's *Amelia* followed *Tom Jones* in 1751. While Fielding wrote this last novel he had been at once an ailing and, as a Westminster magistrate, a very busy man, and though the book shows no descent in feeling, it does show a certain decline in force. Amelia, the heroine, is a married woman, constantly tried but never disillusioned by the weaknesses of her husband, Captain Billy Bond. Her patience, with its triumphant saneness, on the whole suffers less than poor Billy's conscience—sporadic though that conscience may be.

I have given to Fielding and Richardson what may seem by the end of this book to be too much space. But surely they are important ? Not only are they our two innovators, but it seems to me that, in their different work, all later English novels are present in embryo. These two represent two opposed, but equally real, aspects of the English temperament—in a sense, all succeeding English novelists descend from one or other of them. Also, these two men, by the time that their work was finished, had sent out like a challenge their sense of the novel's power, and had shown, without attempting to limit, what was likely to be the English novel's scope. I am sorry that, because of my use of space, I shall not be able to do anything like justice to Tobias Smollett, the Scotsman who, born in 1721, published his *Roderick Random* in 1748—the same year as *Clarissa*.

Of Smollett, it may be said briefly, that he perfected the picaresque romance—he had all the stuff for this, for, disappointed in his early hopes as a dramatist, he had, a navy doctor, gone to sea. After five years of

TOBIAS SMOLLETT 1721-1771
Oil painting by an unknown Italian artist

adventure he returned to London, where he set up as a surgeon in Downing Street. *Roderick Random*, with its attractive hero and quick-moving scenes, obtained a success that justified him in trusting his fortune to his pen. Smollett was—as far as I know—the first novelist to attempt to define the novel. "A novel," he says in one of his dedications, "is a large diffused picture, comprehending the characters of life, disposed in different groups and exhibited in various attitudes, for the purposes of a uniform plan. . . This plan," he adds, "cannot be executed with propriety, probability, or success, without a principal personage to attract the attention, unite the incidents, unwind the clue of the labyrinth, and at last close the scene, by virtue of his own importance." One criticism of Smollett is that his heroes fail to unite the incidents in the novels that they so often name—the incidents being too various for any one character to unite. He has, again,

19

been accused of coarseness. In reality, the touchy, difficult Scotsman (few people knew him well) had a more delicate stomach than his contemporaries : the brutality that was the dark side of our Age of Reason inspired a sort of nausea in him—his reactions were the reactions of nausea. He excelled, perhaps overreached himself, in burlesque. . . . His *Peregrine Pickle* came in 1751, *Ferdinand, Count Fathom* in 1753, and his last and best novel, *Humphry Clinker*, with its postillion hero, in 1771. He admitted he owed much to foreign influences, to Cervantes and to Lesage's *Gil Blas*. His great lack, as an artist, was equanimity. And he bred, through no fault of his own, a most regrettable host of imitators, who threatened again to bring the name of the novel down.

The subtlety lacking in Smollett was brought to a fine point in Laurence Sterne. Born in 1713, at Clonmel in Ireland, son of a poor lieutenant, Sterne, upon leaving Cambridge, took holy orders. During his twenty years' cure of a Yorkshire parish his cloth did not debar him from the enjoyment of privileged eccentricity : he fiddled, shot, had a circle of wild friends, wrote sermons, and all the time revolved a number of matters in the white heat of his curious intellect. The result was to be *Tristram Shandy* —written in Yorkshire, published in London 1759. Contemporary London, dazzled, hardly knew what to think, and we hardly know how to speak now, of this unique book. *Tristram Shandy* bears no intellectual date. It is dementedly natural in its course, surrealist in its association of images. One does not attempt to "follow" *Tristram Shandy* ; one consigns oneself, dizzily, to it. This seems all the odder, because the plot —in so far as there is any plot—is static. The characters—Mr. and Mrs. Shandy, Uncle Toby, Corporal Tim, Yorick the parson, the dapper doctor —stand still, but soar and enlarge from their roots like trees. Young Tristram spends much of his time as an embryo : by the end of the book he is about five years old. The Widow Wadman's appearance is brief and fatal. One may say that, in the pages of *Tristram Shandy*, one finds the whole of English fantasy charted—and what a fantasy! This is a book that inspires volumes : one cannot do much with it in a paragraph. Some people hate Sterne : they say he is maddening and indecent. He is indecent : whether he is maddening depends on you. . . . In 1768 he published the *Sentimental Journey*—a fluid, delicious, capricious and on the whole "easier" book.

Dr. Johnson's *Rasselas*, not exactly a novel, left its impressive mark on the century. It was Johnson who, through an act of kind interference, brought to light the distracted Goldsmith's *Vicar of Wakefield*. Oliver Goldsmith, born in Ireland 1728, and educated at Trinity College, Dublin, had come grimly poor to London, after a series of Continental adventures, only to find a grimmer poverty there. The manuscript of *The Vicar of Wakefield* had moved about with his person, in and out of debtors' prisons, for some years : when the book did come to be published, in 1766, the

FRONTISPIECE TO FANNY BURNEY'S *EVELINA*
Engraving by Mortimer from the edition of 1791

author still maintained in his preface, "There are an hundred faults in this thing." He can but have felt, however, how his book's spirit transcends possible faults. With *The Vicar of Wakefield*, the eighteenth century's first note of intimate tenderness has been struck. Here is true virtue—humble and tried. The Primrose family, with their innocence, their hopes and fears, their lyrical domesticity, exist in an element that seems hardly literature, so unlike is this to the air of another book. Here are the beauty and pathos of youthfulness—the Vicar himself seems hardly old. And when poor lovely Olivia stoops to folly, never did such true sadness surround a fall. As to writing—Goldsmith is the most delicate narrative stylist the

21

eighteenth century put out. He adds to Defoe's directness a poetic lucidity of his own. His comic sense has something rueful about it—all the same, he adds, with the figure of Mrs. Primrose, to the English gallery of great silly women. Mrs. Shandy was there before her ; Mrs. Bennet is to join her soon. With this gem, *The Vicar of Wakefield*, the first great age of the English novel closed.

But the age has a footnote, or epilogue, that one must not miss. Miss Fanny Burney, though only born, at King's Lynn, Norfolk, in 1752, by which year Fielding and Richardson had already finished their best work, comes in time to contribute the woman's view of the Age of Reason and its society. In view of the prejudice against lady writers, Miss Burney not only published anonymously but wrote in secrecy and with some sense of guilt. However, Dr. Johnson's approval was later to justify her career. She was sheltered and nicely bred—the daughter of a doctor of music, whose move with his family up to London added interest to without ever disturbing the tenor of his domestic life—and when she wrote her two most successful novels she still knew little directly of the world. She, however, contemplates scenes of callousness that amount to brutality with just that equanimity Smollett lacked.

Fanny Burney lived to be Queen Charlotte's attendant at the secluded Court, to be chased round Kew Gardens by poor King George III in one of his fits of maniac playfulness, to record all this in a lively journal, and to marry and share the misfortunes of a French émigré, M. D'Arblay. Perhaps real life a little diminished her, for her early work is her best— as having the freshness of someone who still expects much from experience. This freshness endears to us her young heroines. She is not a great novelist—her men are flat figures, though expertly cut out, and her women lack what she lacked : intellect, passion, irony—but she is an engaging, ingenious, often convincing one. *Evelina*, her first novel, published 1778, is the story of *A Young Lady's Entrance into the World*, with the vicissitudes —largely aggressions by vulgar people—that attended it. Fanny Burney's heroines, unlike Jane Austen's, seldom rise above those social miseries that it is their creator's special joy to describe. Could Evelina, for instance, had she found herself in Clarissa Harlowe's position, have suffered more than she does in being seen about with the awful Branghtons ? One doubts it. A subtle falseness of values impairs Fanny Burney's novels, for all their charm. In *Cecilia*, following *Evelina*, this weakness more plainly appears. Burney women, though they protest and blush, are made up of tacit acceptances. A *roué* could have seen Woman in these feminine novels and felt few stirrings of self-reproach ; he could ask, "Can one fundamentally wrong Woman, when she is not able to feel fundamental wrong ?" The ardent spirit in woman had been already saluted by Fielding and Richardson : Jane Austen and the Brontës were later to make its voice heard.

JANE AUSTEN 1775-1817
Engraving after the water-colour drawing by her sister Cassandra Austen

WE must take it that now, for a few decades, the first great English impulse towards the novel, the social impulse, seemed to come to a pause. Already a revolt against Reason, and against its controlling effects, seemed to be on its way. The escape from society, this time, was not to be to the green glades of Arcadia but to the haunted castle and beetling crag. Fancy, so long kept down, now violently reasserted itself. Horace Walpole's *The Castle of Otranto* (1764) was followed by a whole spate of horrific-fantastic tales, featuring demon lovers, shrieks, vaults. This gothic sub-literature is a specialist's subject : I have only room here to name two of its practitioners, Monk Lewis and Mrs. Radcliffe—who closed the century with her *Mysteries of Udolpho* (1794). This crude opening of a romantic revival is, however, important, and must be noted : in it appears that shadowy, deep underneath of the English nature—a nature of which, in the great eighteenth-century novels, we have so far seen only the daylit, orderly top. (Though the dark has already come up

23

through Richardson, with his "brown nodding horrors of elms and pines.") We shall observe how the nineteenth-century novelists attempted to keep in balance the English darkness and day. Apart from its gothic movement, the novel now tended to lapse and fall into disrepute. In quality it grew vapid ; in quantity it was overproduced. Extravagant sensibility gave it its strongest colour ; it was felt to threaten the not strong fortress of reason in a generation of Lydia Languishes.

JANE AUSTEN seems to belong to no century. Her "modernity" has been commented on—which is, I suppose, an agreeable way of saying that she is still some distance ahead of us. I have, earlier, coupled her name with Fielding's : she is like him in her feeling for comedy, her highness of spirit, and, most of all, in so completely not being a muff. She was born in 1775, in Hampshire, at Steventon, of which her father was rector, and her earlier novels were written, though not published,within the bounds of the eighteenth century. Publication dates—Sense and Sensibility, 1811 ; Pride and Prejudice, 1813 ; Mansfield Park, 1814 ; Emma, 1816 ; Persuasion with Northanger Abbey, 1818 (after her death)—do not represent her novels' actual order in her working life. Persuasion was, in fact, her last novel, but Northanger Abbey—which owes its initial satiric idea to Mrs. Radcliffe, as Joseph Andrews owed its to Richardson—had been written as far back as 1798, and Pride and Prejudice, under another title, was the first of her published novels to be written—in 1797, when she was twenty-two.

Herself a delighted reader of novels, Jane Austen saw no reason, and was to show no reason, why the novel should lapse from that place of honour that Fielding and Richardson gained for it. Her own and, I think, only explicit defence of the novel is to be come on early in Northanger Abbey, and here the spirit matches the irony. "Yes, novels," she says, ". . . performances which have only genius, wit and taste to recommend them." She took up her own pen, however, in no dogmatic spirit. She wrote, at her edge of the family parlour table, with just that zest for the scene and joy in discrimination with which she chose new ribbons, flirted and danced. But her genius was imperative. She surrounded each subject she took up with every feeling and faculty that she had. There has been a tendency to accept Jane Austen as no more than a faultless practitioner of the minute : her own remark (to a too fervent clergyman) about the two inches of ivory has been held against her. It is true that she made no effort to pass, through art, outside the range of her own, a gentlewoman's, experience : her novels depict the lives of leisured young men and women in country houses or on visits to Bath or London. Men (and women) in action were her subject, and with her vivid precision she placed action where, by the chance of her birth, she most often saw it—in drawing-rooms and ballrooms, on lawns, in shopping streets. But what she at once depicted and penetrated was not just *a* world, it was *the* world. She arrived at, and was able to fix for us, the denominators of desire, self-delusion and passion that are common to every kind of human experience. Her view of life, in fact, if confined to, was not confined by, drawing-rooms and lawns. She applies big truths to little scenes—so no scene stays "little" under her hand. The constraints of polite behaviour serve only to store up her characters' energies ; she dispels, except for the very stupid, the fallacy that life with the lid off—in thieves' kitchens, prisons, taverns and brothels—is necessarily more interesting than life with the lid on. It is true she has drawn no rebels : her people expect, and derive, pleasure from the straight-forward living of life. But they plan ; they seek, with degrees of determination, ideal circumstances, ideal relationships inside that world they already know. They locate, and never far from themselves, possible darkness, chaos ; they feel the constant threat of the wrong—be this only a mean act, a callous or a designing remark, a subtly deceiving proposition, a lie. The world Jane Austen creates remains an absolute world because of its trueness to its own scale.

Not only the charm but the strength of Jane Austen's novels resides in their being so innately grown-up. In enjoying the youthfulness of her women—most youthful of all in their mistakes—we are at the same time conscious of something in them that remains ageless and poised. So high is this norm of maturity that infantilism, in one form or another, appears as the root of all faults and absurdities : it is imperfect grown-upness that makes people brag, fuss, prattle, play-act or flatter themselves. Among the heroines, poise appears most in her first, Elizabeth Bennet, and in her last, Anne Elliot. But also, Emma Woodhouse retains a lovable balance throughout her headstrong career, and deluded, naïve little Catherine Morland keeps not only Henry Tilney's but the reader's respect. Fanny Price and Elinor Dashwood remain just a shade too sober for many tastes. But one must see that Fanny's sobriety gives much to the structure of *Mansfield Park*, while Elinor acts as the counterpoise to unstable, brilliant Marianne. . . . Jane Austen has also been criticised for an imperfect evaluation of love : it is said that her leisurely, civilised young creatures deny to the passion its true place. She was a great supporter of the rational passion, and the young men allowed to inspire this in her brilliant and her fastidious women are not—with the major exceptions of Mr. Darcy and volatile Henry Tilney—men whom one feels would inspire much. Her tempting alternatives to reason—Willoughby, Frank Churchill, Henry Crawford—are always better done. But, as against this, with what gallant sparkling composure, almost Shakespearean, her heroines' flirtations are conducted, and with what fineness the early shades of attraction are recognised ! Silence always falls on couples of plighted lovers—as though feeling paused outside a door. And, *Persuasion*—could there be a deeper picture of a woman loving too late, apparently without hope ?

Technically—that is, as to matters of form, plot, characterisation, dialogue, setting—Jane Austen remains the most nearly flawless of English novelists. She could not have been other than English—yet she stands a little apart from other writers we have in an artistry that no sentiment blurred, no theory narrowed and no rancour or prejudice side-tracked.

BORN, north of the Border, four years before Jane Austen—in fact, in 1771—Sir Walter Scott was to release England's imagination. Desire for exaltation, love of strangeness, had so far given birth only to gothic tales : Jane Austen had ridiculed mystery. Scott's majestic narrative poems—*The Lay of the Last Minstrel*, 1805 ; *Marmion*, 1808 ; *The Lady of the Lake*, 1810—had first made England look North, and look North with awe. One was met by a landscape dark with clouds and feeling, charged with the past, lost battles, old memories and relentless dreams, a landscape against which the human figure could only stand out in heroic acts. England, who long ago with the Stuarts had accepted a line of Scottish kings, now began to drink in the Scottish tradition—a tradition that returned Fate to its place. (Eighteenth-century England, in common with most of rational Europe, had up to now stressed will rather than fate.) Scott, when he turned to the novel, showed the first great impulse that owed nothing to the sense of society—though it owed everything to the sense of race. What Scott did for his own country in giving voice to its nature is Scotland's and not England's affair : what is certain is that he rushed in on England to fill an emotional vacuum. For the mannered, dry-witted age of the Regency, Jane Austen perfected the novel of manners but this same age received, as though it were parched, Scott's novels that rolled down on it like rain-clouds. And about the man himself there was something warm and commanding that seemed to mellow the air.

The first of his novels, *Waverley*, appeared in 1814—same year as *Mansfield Park*. *Guy Mannering* followed in 1815 ; *The Antiquary* shared 1816 with *Emma*. From then on, the Scott novels are too numerous and regular to enumerate ; outstanding names and dates are : *The Heart of Midlothian* (1818), *The Bride of Lammermoor* (1819), *Ivanhoe* (1820), *Kenilworth* (1821), *Peveril of the Peak* (1822), *Quentin Durward* (1823), *Redgauntlet* (1824), *Woodstock* (1826), *The Fair Maid of Perth* (1828). *Count Robert of Paris* and *Castle Dangerous*, his last two short novels, appeared in 1832—the year of his death.

The idea of the historical novel was in itself, to the England of that day, new. Novelty, linked with its own outstanding power, secured for *Waverley* immediate success. The past, with its accumulation of feeling, was presented with the likeliness of the present day. And when Scott dealt with his own day, as in *Guy Mannering* and *The Antiquary*, past-like emotion gave depth to the scene. He was less happy when, as a *tour de force*, he adventured—as in *Ivanhoe*, *The Talisman*, *Kenilworth*—into English history : reconstruction here is too obvious ; the scenes seem to be cardboard, the people thin. He cut his art off, in fact, from its natural source when he detached himself from his own native mystery. He was truly creative only in regard to his own land. His people are epic figures or nothing, and he could see the epic only in people he instinctively knew. So his novels have their own psychic atmosphere.

Most of the plots contain some major heroic passion. The characters range from great to lowly—many are simple, wanderers, naïve narrative talkers, the trustful, the half-crazed. Scott's treatment of sexual love is stilted—less dishonest than shy. Love with him is always involved with some other aspect of fate. His style depends on emotion for force and lift; so that, when at times the emotion behind it lapses, one feels let down, and resents the verbosity. But such a style, with its poetic richness, was bound, coming when it did, to fecundate English prose. I am less concerned · to claim Scott's Scottish novels for England than to show their effect on the English novelists.

The effect was, on the whole, a loosening one. As such, it was strongly resisted by William Makepeace Thackeray, who, son of a British official in India, had been born near Calcutta in 1811. Thackeray vowed himself to the anti-heroic. Consciously unfortunate Victorian, he was preyed upon by nostalgia for the eighteenth century—seldom does a nostalgia set in so soon. With him it was a case of "Of thee I dream. . . ." Not only did he regret his own place in time, but he is said to have felt that he could have written better had he not been English : this seems strikingly true. Also, much happened to damp down in Thackeray anything like a spontaneous love of life—having received a gentleman's education, and formed along with that a gentleman's ample tastes, he lost his money and was condemned for some time to a seedy existence abroad : when he married, his wife became insane after four years. He lacked the resilience of Fielding, whom he so much admired ; and in his attempts at realism he was infected, more than he may have realised, by the insincerities of his period.

Need to repair his fortunes in the first place drove Thackeray to the pen. He had been writing for papers for some years, under varying pseudonyms and with increasing success, when *Vanity Fair*, with his own name on the covers, began to appear in monthly parts in the year 1847-8—all but a hundred years after *Tom Jones*. This first and great novel of Thackeray's creates for itself an epoch. It was an ambitious book that had not failed. Prodigal in incident, character, sense of period, saturated in humour, spontaneous in its criticism of life, it is in form, at the same time, absolutely controlled. Possibly Thackeray's natural bent was to write about wicked people rather than good. The *Vanity Fair* characters, stamped with life for ever, are headed by that great bad girl Becky Sharp, whose career across other lives her creator follows with a submerged laugh and, I think, some submerged love. The good—through their imperfect virtue —are fooled : Thackeray sees the vice in a sentiment. The length and variety of the book—there is everything in it from a good-bye to a girl's school to drama before the battle of Waterloo—are part of its merit : it suited Thackeray's powers to take a panoramic view of experience. He here uses perfectly his astringent style. The sub-title is *A Novel without a Hero*—and, in fact, there is no one central character, and nobody that one is enjoined to admire ; he gave the book a moral rather than human plan. But this does not make it either abstract or cold. *Vanity Fair* is entrancing, engaging from first to last.

What happened to Thackeray after this ? His powers, after *Vanity Fair*, seem to me to have horribly misdirected themselves. His conceptions remain spacious, his style sometimes masterly and always efficient. But I think he made a mistake in abandoning the complete moral detachment of *Vanity Fair*. In attempting to put across "good" people, in attempting to make disillusionments a matter of tragedy rather than comedy, he commits himself to a sentimentality that is at once laboured and insincere. His anti-heroicism involves every character in the same tepid atmosphere. His *Esmond* (1852) is important as being the first *English* historical novel : the period of the story is Queen Anne. Thackeray, steeped in the Augustine Age, could now give his nostalgias rein : Steele, Swift, Addison walk and talk through the pages—but they seem to creak. In fact, throughout *Esmond* one gets the feeling that damp has got into the works. The triangular situation between Esmond, Lady Castlewood and her daughter Beatrix is boldly conceived but timidly handled—Thackeray may have had this in mind when he implied that he would have liked to be French.

Pendennis (1848) had preceded *Esmond* ; *The Newcomes* (1853-5) followed it. These two novels are interesting as documents of Thackeray's own class—the upper-middle—and age—the early Victorian. They contain some portraits of detestable women, fatally well drawn. *Pendennis*, *The Newcomes* are shells of great novels—or should one say great shells of novels ? But life—and surely they once had life ? seems to have evaporated from them. Over good Colonel Newcome does anybody survive who could shed a tear ? . . . No, the loose rich romantic fullness of Scott certainly did nothing to Thackeray.

As an acknowledged influence on Dickens, I do not remember having heard Scott named—but there must have been something propitious to Dickens's temperament in the atmosphere Scott had left behind. Dickens's subjects are as superficially prosaic as Scott's are evidently poetic, but romantic energy is common to both. Charles Dickens was born at Portsmouth in 1812—a year after Thackeray. His father was a dockyard clerk whose character was to be idealised into Mr. Micawber ; his mother is said to have inspired Mrs. Nickleby. Such an alliance was not likely to

'I AM HOSPITABLY RECEIVED BY MR. PEGGOTTY'
An illustration to Dickens's *David Copperfield*
Engraving by H. K. Browne ("Phiz")

make for domestic stability : the family tottered along and now and then crossed the line that divides fecklessness from declared ruin. After a move to London there came a crash, and little Charles, as a debtor's visiting son, became familiar with the Marshalsea debtors' prison.   To support himself, the boy of twelve worked in a blacking factory, filling and labelling pots.   His father's release from prison set him free to attend a seedy school ; he picked up enough learning to make himself into a solicitor's clerk. Later he taught himself shorthand, and, as reporter for several papers, sat in the gallery of the House of Commons.   This was to be only one phase of his career as a journalist.   He knocked about England, saw and tackled life, drew conclusions, collected fantastic facts.   All his youth he had been an omnivorous reader ; his feeling for "story" had been developed young.   So he wrung the most out of every experience : nothing that happened to Dickens went to waste.   The class from which Dickens sprang—the English shabby-genteel, holding tight to the fringe of respectability—had been up to now ignored by art and society.   It was the pathetic product of an age ruled by commercial ideas of success, in which human values were crude and on the whole mean.   England was still unwilling to cope with the bad conditions industrialism created.   Can one

wonder at Dickens's exaltation—call it sentimental—of the good heart ?
Can one wonder at his tenderness for the devices of fancy by which under-
dog people manage to live ? The sociological aspect of Dickens I have not
got room to discuss here. But remember that he had first been thrust into,
and had later explored by his own will, abysses of injustice and human waste.
Though success met him early—in fact, with the publication of the *Pickwick
Papers*, in monthly parts, in 1836—he never ceased to feel what he had
seen. The buoyancy of his spirits did not make him a less implacable
moralist. He brought up his picturesque, persuasive, sometimes extravagant art against the well-fed callousness that comes largely from lack of
imagination—and he did live to see some reforms. He chose to appeal to
feeling rather than thought—he *was* violently sentimental : leave it at that.
But defiantly, perhaps involuntarily, what an artist he was! There is something superbly childish—I mean, unspoilt—about his imagination. He
gives a child's value—a poor child's—to the enjoyment of sheer physical
bliss—warm lit rooms, trustworthy faces, the roar of a fire, the succulence
of a chop. At the same time, he keeps a child's apprehensiveness of the
weird, the unknown, the unsubstantially threatening. He gives loneliness,
sense of loss or sense of betrayal all the frightful force they have for a child.
Though he draws unconvincing or sugary pictures of "straight" love, he
is first-rate at depicting the sinister attachment—such as Rosa Dartle's to
Steerforth—also, in the depiction of hero-worship. In fact, into all the
love affairs in his books a queer adolescent strain of hero-worship, or
idealisation, enters on one or the other side. His linked senses of threat
and of friendliness make him second to no other writer in penetrating the
atmospheres of landscapes, houses and streets. And he is frightening in
his sense of the power of all kinds of obsession and fantasy.

He was too much embroiled with his subject to be detached in his
style. But his emotional vision sometimes produces the most mobile kind
of English romantic prose. Read, for instance, the passage beginning
"The waters are out in Lincolnshire . . ." in Chapter II. of *Bleak House*.
Bleak House (1852-3) seems to me the most impressive, *David Copperfield*
(1849-50) the most august and tender, and *Great Expectations* (1860-1)
the most original of Dickens's novels. But no name of a novel of his is
unknown, and few of his novels, I think, remain unread. In him the
English genius finds a wide course : he is as comprehensive as any writer
we have. His zest and humour have been likened to Fielding's. But he
has in common with Richardson his perception of the nervous, or dusky,
side of the human make-up.

When Dickens died, he left unfinished a mystery story, *Edwin Drood*.
His growing preoccupation with mystery was due to his friendship with
Wilkie Collins, who, born in 1824, was to do brilliantly in this genre.
Wilkie Collins, in fact, may be called the grandfather of the English
detective story. He had not only a great sense of human drama but a

A LITERARY GATHERING IN 1844
Charles Dickens reading *The Chimes* to his friends in Forster's chambers
Pencil drawing by Daniel Maclise

command, to be envied, of "atmospheric" style—see the description of the tree-muffled Hampshire mansion at midnight, and of the dead lake, in *The Woman in White*. He also created—as in Count Fosco—superbly sinister figures, and drew some unforgettable scenes. His two greatest stories are *The Woman in White* (1860) and *The Moonstone* (1868).

Anthony Trollope, another friend of Dickens, has only lately come into his own again. Less intellectual and fastidious but also less arid than Thackeray, more stolid and less fantastic than Dickens, he seems to me the most sheerly able of the English Victorian novelists. He was honest enough about his own age to be able to give an objective picture of it ; he was less affected by pruderies than prepared to make discreet allowance for them. One cannot deny that, with the nineteenth century, a sort of fog did begin, in the English novel, to obscure some vital aspects of life. It became more difficult to write greatly because it became less possible to write truly. There was facetiousness on the subject of class, squeamishness on the subject of sex. One could no longer travel straight across country, as the eighteenth-century novelists had done. Evasions made for sentimentality. Anthony Trollope probably recognised that, for the Victorian novelist, absolute integrity was impossible ; but he made towards an integrity of his own. . . . Born in 1815, three years after Dickens, he had an unhappy childhood (see his *Autobiography*) : he seemed to himself to be born at a disadvantage—which makes one all the more admire the

CHARLOTTE BRONTË 1816-1855
Chalk drawing by George Richmond

saneness with which he reconciled himself with life. First as a clerk, then as a civil servant (travelling in the pay of the Post Office), he had had usefully varied experience : he got to know all grades of society and to enjoy the stretch of the English scene. The geniality that he arrived at breathes never speciously, through his novels—whose increasing success made him able to leave the Post Office and give to his new profession his full time. He wrote hard, and under prosaic conditions.

Trollope is most remembered for his clergymen : in the famous Barsetshire novels he seals up for ever the atmosphere and the personalities of an English cathedral town. He immortalised also English squires, peers, professional people and politicians. Also, I know few writers better than Trollope at conveying the charm of a charming scene. Many of his comedy characters—for instance, the incorrigible Bertie of *Barchester Towers*—are first rate. He can—as in *The Warden*—at once honour and analyse the English conscience at its most austere. He has the merit of being a very masculine writer. If he fought shy of passion, he created

SIR WALTER SCOTT 1771-1832
Oil painting by Sir Thomas Lawrence

WILLIAM MAKEPEACE THACKERAY 1811-1863
Oil painting by John Gilbert

MRS. GASKELL 1810-1865
Chalk drawing by George Richmond

women who could inspire it : he puts the English heroine back on the map again ; his young women are lovely, ardent, intelligent, capable, true. In some of them—especially Mary Thorne—the gallant spirit once more appears. After several early tries at the novel, Trollope arrived with *The Warden* (1855). The rest of the Barsetshire novels followed. He embarked with *Phineas Finn* (1869) on a political series—less well known now because less well done : Disraeli was far better in this genre. In *Can You Forgive Her ?* (1864) he tackled the subject of erring womanhood. Before he died he had written sixty novels in all.

T HE Brontë genius remains a phenomenon of all, not only of English, literature. Haworth vicarage, exposed on the wilds of Yorkshire, was the home of this family : pilgrims now gaze around the vicarage as though the force of the Brontë living must have left its mark on these darkish walls. The Rev. Patrick Brontë had come from the North of

Ireland : of his marriage, in 1812, there were six children—two daughters who died at a boarding-school for the daughters of clergymen, then Charlotte (1816), Patrick Branwell, Emily (1818), Anne (1820). By 1822 the family were motherless : poverty, isolation, very delicate health made up the medium of their existences. As children they roamed the moors. Charlotte went for some time to the school—the Lowood of *Jane Eyre*— that had killed her sisters. Branwell—a character so sinister that he started a darker part of the Brontë legend—took drugs, wasted money and kept the family feeling at burning point. The sisters went out as governesses : Charlotte and Emily, in order to learn languages, attached themselves for a time to the Pensionnat Héger, in Brussels. In 1846 the three sisters together published *Poems by Currer, Ellis and Acton Bell*. Charlotte's first novel, *The Professor*, failed to find a publisher, but in 1847 *Jane Eyre*, "by Currer Bell," appeared. And in that same year came *Wuthering Heights* by the "Ellis Bell" who was Emily. Anne Brontë published two gentler novels, *Agnes Grey* and *The Tenant of Wildfell Hall*. By the close of 1849 Branwell, Emily and Anne were dead—it was a wonder that they had lived so long. Charlotte, in that year, published *Shirley ; Villette*, a reconstruction of *The Professor*, appeared in 1853. A year later she married her father's curate, but she was to die in 1855. *The Professor* was published after her death. Old Mr. Brontë was left alone at Haworth : none of his children had reached the age of forty.

But it is an ageless fire that burns in the novels the Brontës left. The sisters were young chiefly in having lost none of their vehemence ; they were involved with little outside themselves—only Charlotte at all came to terms with life. Emily, having consumed her own lonely experience, translated experience to an unearthly plane. *Wuthering Heights* is a book of fire and ice : no book has ever been better named. It is raged through, as by a wind, by a damned soul—the fated, fatal Heathcliff. The love in it is relentless, as pure of hope as it is of flesh. The house is solitary, exposed . . . . here is the real English dark tower of passion above all rationality. All the same, the material setting is circumstantial; the story is full of pictures stored in Emily's living eye—the feathers plucked from the pillow, the two children in the tree in the wind. The Thrushcross firelight, with its domestic promise, by contrast darkens the darkness that is the lovers' home. And the love of Heathcliff and Catherine gains in poetic intensity by being set back inside a complex prosaic form—much of the narrative is in the idiom of "ordinary" people ; the consternation of limited people frames the unlimited tragedy.

Wuthering Heights bears no definite feminine stamp—though perhaps only a woman could have liberated her spirit so completely. Charlotte Brontë's *Jane Eyre*, on the other hand, gains force by being woman from beginning to end. Made in this voice, the plain, proud, unhesitating assertion of woman's feeling for man—Jane's for Rochester—shocked the

34

'OUR SOCIETY'
An illustration by Hugh Thomson to Mrs. Gaskell's *Cranford*

England of 1847. It had been the accepted idea that, while woman might, by very judicious degrees, respond to declared love, she did not initiate love on her own account—to do so was more than doubtful, it was "unwomanly." So *Jane Eyre*, in spite of its actually faultless morals, took on an odour of impropriety—which is not to say that it was not read. If Jane, the plain little sprite of a governess, does not court her employer Rochester, she challenges him in Cleopatra's voice : their scene in the July dusk of the garden is unforgettable. Jane wants much more than love ; she wants human fullness of life—the book voiced, for the first time, woman's demand for this. Read the scene where, alone on the roof of the country house, Jane looks out over the country and cries for movement, achievement, adventure—feeling the masculine part of her spirit stir. Might this be called the first feminist novel ? The nature of her struggle with Rochester, who, when his existing marriage has been discovered, wants her to be his mistress, shows the hundred years' difference between Jane and Clarissa. But Jane, like Clarissa Harlowe, still identifies virtue with the power to keep her fate in her own hands. . . . *Jane Eyre*, set nearer to every-day life than *Wuthering Heights*, has a few social improbabilities in which the Brontë lack of worldly experience shows. Temperamental black-whiskered Rochester may fall a prey to our laughter ; the black-souled Heathcliff never does. Charlotte Brontë, naïve, starved of beauty and luxury, rather over-describes gilded scenes—the drawing-room lit for a party, the harpy charmer's veneer. But there is something endearing about this weakness of hers. In *Shirley* she also portrays glamour—the glamour of Shirley's dashing temperament. After *Jane Eyre*, *Villette*—with its foreign atmosphere of waxed floors and cold windows, the romantic rigidity of the boarding school—is her best book. . . . At a time when male approval, coupled with money, gave woman the only status she had, it is remarkable that the only giant novels should have been written by spinster daughters of an obscure indigent clergyman.

After the Brontës, George Eliot—really Mary Ann Evans—may seem opaque and pedestrian. Not for nothing did she assume a masculine name. Her intellect must be honoured—it is more constructive than brilliant—her emotion is gravely coloured by it. She was at grips with the problems of her day. If not an attractive, she was a great, woman : as an artist she is never to be despised. Born in 1819, daughter of a land-agent, she, in helping her father with his business, early took a hand in practical life. Courageous in her emotions, she lived for years in free union with George Henry Lewes—not the least of a group of advanced thinkers to whom her propensities had attracted her. Experience had made her know many people ; imagination made her penetrate them. Provincial-Midland-England is the scene of her best books—and, above all, she knew the yeoman class. She had her own sense of beauty—best seen in *Middlemarch* (1871), *Scenes from Clerical Life* (1858), and *The Mill on the Floss* (1860). She had humour, but is greatest in tragedy, which with her is found more in character (with its misuse or vain sacrifices of will) than in fate. *Felix Holt the Radical* was, in 1866, the rather stark intellectual high-point of her career. For the emotional interest one expects from a novel she is best in *Adam Bede* (1859) and *Silas Marner* (1861). She can write with a faultless convincingness, and with a noble sweep of imagination—apart from this, her books, with their palpable truth to life, are important as documents of their day.

All the same, in my heart I prefer Mrs. Gaskell—as sincere a person, a less major artist and a more feminine soul. Born in 1810, she had been a beautiful Chelsea girl, reared on a succession of country visits. She married a Unitarian minister and lived, worked and felt with him in Manchester, among "the dark satanic mills." Her reaction to the injustices she found in industrial England of that day was of the heart, but was ruled by her steady head : unlike Dickens, she never overpainted ; truth seemed to her good, and bad, enough. She never lost her love—and perhaps her nostalgia—for the sweet, the comely, the orderly, the agreeable, though these, to warrant her love, must be founded on moral right. Happy in her own life as a woman, she was keenly aware of injustices done to her sex in the name of morality—she wrote her bold *Ruth* in 1853. Before this had come *Mary Barton, a Tale of Manchester Life* (1848), which is a document of the Chartist year. Called the first "labour" novel, it prays for improved understanding between masters and men. *North and South* is much in the same vein. *Cranford*, that delicious idyll of gentility, appeared the

'GEORGE ELIOT' 1819-1880
Chalk drawing by Sir Frederick W. Burton

same year as *Ruth*—to which it is a counterpoise. It is *Cranford*, with its
immortal old ladies, that keeps Mrs. Gaskell's name so widely known and
loved in the world. Reading *Cranford* after Jane Austen's *Emma*—that
other picture of an enclosed society—one is conscious of the change there
had been in England in the forty years between those two books. Emma
Woodhouse's Highbury is unthreatened ; Miss Matty's Cranford is not—
behind its orderly, small-town silence one feels vibrations from "Drumble"
—the not distant out-spreading Manchester. . . . In the *Wives and
Daughters* she did not live to finish (she died in 1865) Mrs. Gaskell returns
to the Southern scene. With these four Victorian women writers we seem
to come to the close of a period : we pass from the Mid-Victorian to the
Late. The change is, rather, in attitude : the actual dates of authors
overlap.

Several of George Meredith's novels, for instance, were contemporaries
of George Eliot's, and his first, *The Shaving of Shagpat*, appeared only nine
years after *Wuthering Heights*. He was born in 1828—and was to live on

37

into our century. He was of Welsh extraction, and went to a Moravian school in Wales : his grandfather had been a successful tailor—a fact that was to be dug up by those enemies who accused him of snobbery (there was something less arid than snobbery in Meredith's love of the truly grand). On his return from school to London he became a solicitor's clerk, but published his first *Poems* (containing *Love in a Valley*) in 1851. These drew the attention, and later the friendship, of Rossetti and Swinburne to the brilliant young man. In fact, he was able to develop his talents in an atmosphere that was most propitious to them. He became the first English novelist with a conscious aesthetic—this may account for the *hauteur* of his style—and, more, he had a philosophy, as opposed to a general theory of right and wrong.

His poetry provides the key to his novels. Able to leave the solicitor's office for journalism, Meredith, from his room in Rossetti's house, wrote only for papers whose reputation did nothing to damage his promising name. Grub Street never really impinged on him. His first marriage failed : in 1864, one year after his second, he went to live at Flint Cottage, Box Hill, Surrey, which remained his home for the rest of his long life.

As a novelist Meredith has been found obscure, besides being a little too unaware of the banal side of human experience. The complex content of his prose does sometimes choke it—his poetry, on the other hand, continues to burn with intellectual vision. It has been argued that he should have kept to poetry. But his poems—culminating in *Modern Love* and *The Woods of Westermain*—are essentially those of a novelist. And without his novels his smashing intellectual humour, his capricious descriptions would have been lost. Perhaps as a novelist he suffers from having lived too much in an eclectic world—unlike Thackeray, Dickens, Trollope, he can seldom have been mortified or bored. He tends to precipitate his characters—who are themselves, from their start in his brain, dynamic— into rather too special an atmosphere. His novels are, in a sense, too like operas.

All the same, it was Meredith who produced that almost faultless novel *The Egoist* (1879), in which the best of the English comedy spirit flowers— at once satirical and rotund. The plot ?—a high-minded baronet is more truly, less kindly seen by a young lady than was Sir Charles Grandison. Here, too, Meredith perfects, in the best tradition, a purely English scene. One might say that his scenes are more likely, on the whole, than his characters—these, though vivid, being at times out of drawing. His sense of heroic promise in people is shadowed by his sense of their weaknesses : "We are betrayed by what is false within." He adored love, and shows it as adorable—all the same, he sees it as an ordeal—his early *The Ordeal of Richard Feverel* (1859) even takes its title from this idea. His stories about the youngness of young men deal with evolution rather than with adventure. Sometimes he applies his vision to politics, to national aspiration, to the

38

GEORGE MEREDITH 1828-1909
Chalk drawing by William Strang

international scene : some of his novels range far abroad. His heroines
move through Olympian air : one charge against them has been that they
talk too much. In his famous *Diana of the Crossways* (1885) he undertakes
the defence of a noble creature. *Evan Harrington* (1861), *Rhoda Fleming*
(1865), *Vittoria* (1867), *Beauchamp's Career* (1876), *The Amazing Marriage*
(1895) also stand high with Meredith readers. He may be attacked, but he
cannot be overlooked : I feel certain that he will stand the test of time.

Samuel Butler belongs in this period from having been born in 1835.
His reputation, however, has been cumulative, and his importance continues
to grow to-day. Grandson of the great bishop of that same name, he, on
leaving Cambridge, renounced the intention of taking holy orders and went
out to New Zealand, to sheep-farm. Successful in this, he also began to
write. Returning to London he took up painting, and exhibited at the
Royal Academy. It was in 1872 that he published his satire *Erewhon*—
which has been likened to *Gulliver's Travels*. Butler might, indeed, be
called the nineteenth-century Swift—comprehensive, at once enraged and

precise. Grievance—his whole bent was to science, but he held himself to be boycotted by a group of accredited scientists—at once warped him and steeled his curious power. He has many aspects, but comes into the scope of this book because of his one novel, *The Way of All Flesh*. He began this in 1872 ; he laid it aside in 1885—and it was not published till 1903. It is at once a hate-charged and scientific analysis of English middle-class family life (as embodied in the Pontifex family), especially of the relationship between parents and children, and its effects. It was well for the English eighteen-seventies and 'eighties, with their placid system of family reverence, that *The Way of All Flesh*, though in their time being written, was held up and did not explode on them. 1903 was quite soon enough. *The Way of All Flesh*, coming just when it did, has inspired a whole school of iconoclast novels.

Thomas Hardy was born, near the Dorchester he was to rechristen Casterbridge, in 1840, twelve years after Meredith. These two Late-Victorian novelists have in common that they were both poets. But while Meredith might be called a magnificent by-product of the English genius, Hardy is a figure in its direct line. In fact, his is a figure in which many tendencies culminate. The strangeness of his novels—a strangeness as great, at times, as that of *Wuthering Heights*—is counterpoised by their pervasive physical naturalness. He was England's first regional novelist—setting his stories in a tract he called Wessex, that centres on his own county of Dorsetshire. But whereas other regional novelists simply use, Hardy created, local colour : he confers a sort of super-existence on the region he wrote about. It would be true to say that Hardy did for his part of England what Scott had done for the Border. But a whole extension of complex human experience lies between the two. Scott's country people are walking traditions ; Hardy's are sharply individualised : there is not one "type" in the whole of his gallery. Scott revived the dignity of the past ; Hardy, although the past works in him, is moved by a philosophic consciousness of the future.

Of the hero of *The Return of the Native* (1878) he says, for instance : "In Clym Yeobright's face could dimly be seen the typical countenance of the future. Should there be a classic period to art hereafter, its Phidias may reproduce such faces. The view of life as a thing to be put up with, replacing that zest for existence which was so intense in early civilisations, must ultimately enter so thoroughly into the constitution of the advanced races that its facial expression will be accepted as a new artistic departure. People already feel that a man who lives without disturbing a curve of feature, or setting a mark of mental concern upon himself, is too far from modern perceptiveness to be a modern type. . . . The observer's eye was arrested, not by his face as a picture, but by his face as a page ; not by what it was but what it recorded. His features were attractive in the light of symbols. . . ." "The view of life as a thing to be put up with"—what a

THE VISIT TO THE MAD WOMAN AFTER THE INTERRUPTED MARRIAGE

Illustration to *Jane Eyre* by Charlotte Brontë

Water-colour by Frederick Walker

THOMAS HARDY 1840-1928
Oil painting by Augustus John

ong way the human spirit had travelled by the time Hardy wrote that. There is, throughout his feeling for nature, the same sublime awareness of an endurance. Egdon Heath, in the timeless November dusk, as yet crossed by no figure, occupies the first chapter of *The Return of the Native*. 'It was at present a place perfectly accordant with man's nature—neither ghastly, hateful nor ugly : neither commonplace, unmeaning or tame ; but, like man, slighted and enduring, and withal singularly colossal and mysterious in its swarthy monotony."

But meekness is no note of Hardy's characters. His young men and women, each one singularly alone, each raise a kind of cry for perfection—through intellectual or moral achievement, through love. Each one is made dynamic either by a desire or an idea. The most alive of the men are creatures of intellect ; the most alive of the women are creatures of passion. But he has also created the character that is stable and philosophic—born, one might say, already half reconciled. Very often such people are very simple : old lore, inherited wisdom speak through them.

The Return of the Native (1878), *Tess of the D'Urbervilles* (1891), and *Jude the Obscure* (1896), all three of them tragedies, have been recognised as the greatest of Hardy's novels. All have their superhumanly human scenes—Eustacia tending her solitary beacon fire, Tess waking from her bridal sleep to the fatal sunrise of Stonehenge, Jude's love Sue raising her sick husband to see the sunset reflected in a bedroom mirror. Hardy's art is, above all, diverse. His comedy spirit is, therefore, august and mellow. Merry-making, weddings and village dancing, the comic charm of bravado, naïve, racy talk, the emanation of magic from a beautiful woman, the delicious negligent poise of a pretty one, the fine day and the fine fellow, the strong sweep of hope and the long sweep of open country come equally into his range. His style, sublime at its greatest, does sometimes lapse into bathos ; his dialogue, at its best idiomatic, alive with natural rhythm, has reaches of stilted unlivingness. But the architecture of his novels cannot be criticised : it is beyond praise. Hardy, after a meagre education, did in fact qualify and for years practise as an architect—so from one art to another he carried sound rules. And, his conception of life being elemental the poet in him fused with the novelist. His outstanding novels, other than those I have mentioned, are : *Under the Greenwood Tree* (1872), *Far from the Madding Crowd* (1874), *The Mayor of Casterbridge* (1886), *The Woodlanders* (1887).

ENGLAND cannot really claim Henry James, though he claimed England by coming to live here and becoming in 1916 a naturalised Englishman. An American, born in New York State in 1843, he became, while still a young man, familiar with what was civilised in both hemispheres. In their high, wise kind of sophistication, his novels are cosmopolitan. At the same time, he keeps, in his observations, the alert austerity of the pioneer. He writes at once with the detachment of a spectator and the close-upness of someone under a spell. He might be called the analyst of civilisation—and from this point of view England, with its enigmas, its inconsistencies, its puzzling, superb survivals, fascinated him. And, as a novelist, he was fascinated by the phenomenon of the English conscience. His affinities, as an artist in writing, were to artists abroad—Flaubert, Turgeniev—but he was to crown England, at the close of one century and the start of another, with a series of novels that penetrated to the essential Englishness of her scene. One might say that she had not been so completely perceived before.

One may say that James's perceptions only worked in the particular area of his social tastes. He had an aesthetic love of the *beau monde*—whether it be of artists or aristocrats. As in Meredith's case, desire attracted him to the people and settings of which he wrote. Any character in a Henry James story or novel, however low his or her stated class in life, is promoted—by being made articulate or susceptible—to his or her place in James's *beau monde*. And he makes the same promotions in age as he does in class : even his children are, in their fineness, mature. In a sense, his adults are child-like, in having crystalline natures. The fact was, that James could only use the *fine* nature—whether evil or good—for his very special treatment of the predicament. And predicament was his subject, at every time. His sense of beauty is matched by his sense of evil : his villains do worse than oppress or threaten—they subtly and immeasurably corrupt. His innocent characters move through danger zones ; the spirit is in peril, seldom the flesh. Evil only operates quite directly in a few of the James stories—the great example is *The Turn of the Screw*. Elsewhere, its action is indirect ; it may work through the most apparently natural affections, desires and loyalties . . . see, for instance, *The Spoils of Poynton* (1896). In *The Golden Bowl*, with its London scene of poised and controlled cosmopolitan people, he shows the implicit rather than the conventional ugliness of an adultery. Under Henry James's adroitness, behind his complex constructions, is the simple pattern of the morality play. In the end, he sees nothing as beautiful that has not been proved good. He subjected to moral examination the grace, the privilege, the mystery, the tradition of the age-polished England he loved so well.

Henry James's great novels and stories are astoundingly many. His style became more and more involuted ; his later novels are not found easy to read. His first long novel was *Roderick Hudson* (1876). Landmarks in his work have been : *The American* (1877), *Daisy Miller* (1878), *The Portrait of a Lady* (1881), *The Princess Casamassima* (1886), *The Spoils of Poynton* (1896), *What Maisie Knew* (1897), *The Two Magics* (which contains *The Turn of the Screw*) (1898), *The Awkward Age* (1899), *The Wings of the Dove* (1902), *The Ambassadors* (1903), *The Golden Bowl* (1904). Though he did not die (in England) till 1916, his great fiction period had closed years before that.

So Henry James has carried us over from the nineteenth century to our own. The same transition was made by a number of novelists whom, alas, I have no room to name here. In fact, the great Late-Victorians I have discussed were in reality far from isolated : to let them seem so gives an incomplete picture of their day. It has taken years for them to stand out from among their more popular contemporaries. I am now conscious of two very bad lacunæ in not having mentioned either George Gissing or George Moore—the first a "straight" realist, the second an æsthete-realist, Irish, much touched by French influence, whose work has an outstanding quality. And a still graver omission is Robert Louis Stevenson, the second great Scot to influence England. In his power to raise the story of action to a heroic, sometimes poetic, level, Stevenson was to be approached by Joseph Conrad—the Polish sea captain who added to English writing a sort of fervour and glory—a temperament. I can name, in the space that is left to me, only four novelists who carry forward into, or at least touch, our own time.

There is Rudyard Kipling, for instance. The artist in him has been quite wrongly obscured, in some views, by the Imperialist. Actually, he was realistic, quite disabused, about English life abroad as well as at home. The dramatic side of the Empire did appeal to him—but he knew its plain working side well, as a journalist. He likes energy, courage, action in any form : if he salutes these in the English one cannot blame him. His best work is in the field of the short story—setting and incident interest him more than character, though his touch on character can be devastatingly sure. His long novel, *The Light that Failed*, is, though moving, on the sentimental side. No English writer has been more mobile and vivid in his depiction of action. Also, he makes one see, smell, touch what he describes : his descriptions are charged with reality. For a number of untravelled English people he has, for instance, "created" India for ever. He has, and quite often likes to use, a real English-gothic command of the horrific. In *Plain Tales from the Hills*, and other collections, he has written some ruthless love-stories : love does not appear to Kipling to be a rational passion. Anglo-Indian life, boy life and the British Army are, in general, taken to be his province. In his children's stories he shows pure imagination in his treatment of the past and of animals. He was born in Bombay in 1865, and the publication dates of his books extend from 1881 to 1930. He has left us some classic tales of the 1914-18 war.

H. G. Wells, born 1866, has, like Samuel Butler, the scientific approach to life. He applies science to the novel. Like Hardy, he has a constant sense of the future—but, whereas Hardy apprehended the future only as the extreme of a psychic state, Wells commits himself to exact material prophecies. Science has justified his predictions by already coming abreast

43

of several of them—but the stories have their independent place in art as being magnificent fantasies. *The Time Machine*, for instance, came in 1895 *The War of the Worlds* in 1898, *The Food of the Gods* in 1904, *Men Like God* in 1923. It may be said that Wells's rationalised Utopias offer no place for the human soul—which, one takes it, will no longer exist. If so, in the future there will be no more great novels. . . . The Utopian novels have made great impacts : fearless, iconoclastic, impertinent from the point of view of tradition, they do always stimulate thought. But it is in conscious-ness of his own age, of the maladies and the aspirations of men as they are to-day—in fact, as a straightforward novelist—that Wells seems to me to excel. He has a truly Dickensian eye for the comic. *Kipps* (1905) and *The History of Mr. Polly* (1910) are novels that could not be better. *Ann Veronica* (1909), *Marriage* (1912), *Joan and Peter* (1918) are milestones in the analysis of his age. Wells is at once engaged and fascinated by the impossibility of rationalising love : sex seems to hold up progress, the way things are. Others of the novels—outstandingly, *Mr. Britling Sees It Through* (1916)—fall into the document group : they crystallise the feeling and the conditions of a particular period. From the first, Wells has been liked or disliked for a particular boldness—*Tono Bungay* (1909) and *The New Machiavelli* (1911) made revolutions in their day. And the present day has not yet caught up with his thoughts : for our own generation he flies a tremendous flag.

In his move from the social novel, with its acceptances, to the socio-logical novel, with its attacks, Wells was accompanied by Arnold Bennett (1867-1931). But in the Bennett novels—which at their finest, for instance, *The Old Wives' Tale* (1908), stand up to anything Europe has put out—the artist towers over the man of ideas. In fact, general conditions chiefly interested Bennett in so far as they serve to explain particular lives. Like Hardy, he re-created a region—the Five Towns, in the northern Midlands, dark with the smoke of the potteries. In him appears, at its most lively, the English satiric sense—and as success closed in on his own life, how freely he satirised success ! He became accomplished enough as a writer to explore every genre—the thriller, the domestic comedy. After the *Old Wives' Tale*, among his serious work comes the *Clayhanger* trilogy (1910-15), and *Riceyman Steps* (1923). He lived years in France, loved her and learned from her the uncompromising regard that is due to art. The French æsthetic ideal—detachment—was always uppermost in his mind : to this we owe his objective view of England—as valuable in an English-man as it is rare.

John Galsworthy's novels have not worn so well. His dates are 1867-1933. The *Forsyte Saga* novels (1906-28) have their first interest—and are much read abroad—as documents of the English upper middle class. They have the merits of all his other writing—intellectual scrupulousness, sense of beauty, a rather hopeless passion for social justice, and, with regard to

RUDYARD KIPLING 1865-1936
Oil painting by Sir Philip Burne-Jones

women, a serious but exotic sentimentality. His pictures of men of property, men created by their sense of their own position, are more searching than Thackeray's, more fastidious than Trollope's—yet somehow the different Forsytes fail to be major figures. Possibly Galsworthy was not ruthless enough ; perhaps he failed (while he did boldly attempt) to objectify the tradition in which he had been brought up. He attacks privilege, but in a privileged way. His disinterested ambitions deserve praise : one would not be so much aware of his limitations had he not attempted to do so much. As a dramatist—and he was called the English Ibsen—he learned how to give the fullest force to a scene—so it is the scenes in his novels that are remembered ; one tends to lose sight of their continuity. In his sense of place he excels ; he has immortalised London ; he has a sensuous feeling for countrysides. His characters, with their ascetic wills, dread beauty because of its dangerous power : in fact, you could not have a fairer example than Galsworthy of one kind of English romanticism. His novels most to be recommended are : *The Man of Property* (1906), *The*

Patrician (1911), *The Dark Flower* (1913), *In Chancery* (1920), *To Let* (1921).
These four writers—Kipling, Wells, Bennett and Galsworthy—have been in their time, and each in his own way, more revolutionary than any younger men. We now take for granted a great deal that they achieved. The novelist of to-day has less to react against. So we feel some break in temperament between these four last Late-Victorians and the novelists who are at their maturity to-day—for instance, Aldous Huxley, Somerset Maugham. Has there come, too, a break in the English novel tradition ? Looking back, we may say that the English novelists have, from the eighteenth century up to some years ago, excelled in the creation of character. and, secondarily, in the drawing of scenes, rather than in the analysis of ideas and passions. They have left us a gallery of immortal English creatures—eccentrics, haphazard fine young men, fantasists, optimists blackguards, silly women, dashing bad women, lovely spirited girls ; they have left us English landscapes as various as ever came from the sweep of an English brush. Hardy and Meredith, poet-novelists, were the first to indicate any change.

There is, I think, a change now, though not a break. D. H. Lawrence has come and gone : his explosive novels have had the effect of a sort of depth-charge, bringing much to the surface. Lawrence was, it would seem, at once behind and in advance of his own time : his puritanical antipuritanism was paradoxical. In writing of worlds he knew, he commanded an admirable realism, tinged with poetry, and a simplicity that has not been praised enough; these having been obscured, for the general reader, by his "prophetic" quality, and by his (apparent) doctrine of purification by fire—*i.e.*, sexual passion. At any rate, D. H. Lawrence played a major part in shifting the stress from character—in which, ever since, our contemporary novelists show an interest that is much less exclusive. They continue to turn, instead, to just those ideas and passions of which their predecessors fought shy. In this they are not un-English . they are simply returning to an English age before the novel began. In fact, they are more like the Elizabethans—also, they embrace something of the seventeenth-century metaphysic. In their hands, the novel takes a poetic trend. Is this because we live in an age of ideas and passions in which individual destinies count for less, in which people take less colour from their surroundings because those surroundings change from day to day ? One great war has already left, and now another has also placed, its mark on English habit, feeling and thought. I do not think English essentials will ever change—but events make us sharply conscious of what these are. The novelist to-day must think for himself : this is no time to add random comments to life. So the English novel gains in self-consciousness—it may have lost some of the old spontaneity.

I cannot see my contemporaries as I see the earlier novelists : that is I cannot see them down the perspective of time. They are many, and

46

ARNOLD BENNETT 1867-1931
Caricature by David Low

vitally on the move. To attempt to judge them would be to attempt to immobilise them. I may have been arbitrary about the dead ; I will not be misleading about the living. With every day, values go up and down. So I shall close with a reference only to two modern novelists whose work seems to me to have attained a position clear of the daily critical flux. One, Virginia Woolf, is recently dead ; the other, E. M. Forster, has not published a novel since 1924. These two seem to me both to epitomise English tradition and to have moved forward along lines of their own.

E. M. Forster's novels are more straightforward, more (at least apparently) in the familiar manner than those of Virginia Woolf : they have developed plots, they give place (though not the first place) to character ; they have a high ironic level of comedy, and their dialogue comes abreast with Jane Austen's. What is new in them is their particular mental climate ; also, the nature of other people's predicaments. Contrast does much to give these novels structure and meaning—contrast between one country, with its inherent spirit, and another (suburban England and hill-

47

town Italy in *Where Angels Fear to Tread*, between England and India in *A Passage to India*), between convention and passion (in *A Room with a View*), between illusion and truth (in *The Longest Journey* and *Howard's End*). In each, the central character is kept at the high tension of a continuous decision. Through experience the character seems to make a journey—an often lonely destination is reached. The controlled, level style of the narration can be penetratingly beautiful.

In Virginia Woolf's novels the characters are less mobile ; they seem to stand still, amazed, while experience ripples past. The men and women have an intense inner existence ; each generates his or her own world. Imagination of this pure power has not been brought to narrative style before : Virginia Woolf has been likened to Sterne—but her imagination is less contused than his. I have not heard her compared with Emily Brontë—but Emily Brontë has been the only other woman capable of this upward sweep. While the *Wuthering Heights* setting is in itself extraordinary, Virginia Woolf's choice of settings has been the reverse, and her characters are, in their outward aspects, made almost deliberately tame. She chooses, in fact, unlikely matter to kindle—but, once kindled, how high she makes it burn ! She has put behind her, having no need of, devices that make all other stories work. The towering inner strangeness of her people appears not at all in their outward actions (which appear conventional and compliant), but in the manner in which they see and feel. Only in the earliest of her novels, *The Voyage Out*, do the characters actually make a journey : they go to South America. Otherwise, they are confined to the experiences of London, the English countryside and seashore. But never before has England appeared as it appears under this burning-glass of her art. Once, in *Orlando*, she turns the glass on the English past. Otherwise, all her titles—*Night and Day, Jacob's Room, Mrs. Dalloway, To the Lighthouse, The Waves, The Years, Between the Acts*—suggest the familiar "now"—the familiar scene, in cycles of light and darkness, in hearing of the rhythm of tides. Time, not passion, spins any plot that there is —and yet Virginia Woolf has been supreme in her power to place the life art touches beyond the power of time.

I have tried, as I promised at the start of this book, to make felt the wideness of the To-day of art, and return past novelists to their place in its light. So it is fitting to close with Virginia Woolf's name : she lived as well as wrote in the presence of that To-day.

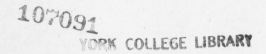